The NFL's Greatest Teams

KANSAS CITY CHIEFS

Katie Lajiness

Big Buddy Books
An Imprint of Abdo Publishing
abdopublishing.com

abdopublishing.com

Published by Abdo Publishing, a division of ABDO, PO Box 398166, Minneapolis, Minnesota 55439.

Printed in the United States of America, North Mankato, Minnesota.
092016
012017

THIS BOOK CONTAINS RECYCLED MATERIALS

Cover Photo: ASSOCIATED PRESS.
Interior Photos: AP (pp. 17, 19); AP Images (p. 6); ASSOCIATED PRESS (pp. 5, 7, 9, 11, 12, 13, 14, 15, 17, 18, 19, 20, 21, 23, 25, 27, 28, 29); NFL photos (p. 11); Tony Tomsic (p. 11).

Coordinating Series Editor: Tamara L. Britton
Graphic Design: Michelle Labatt, Taylor Higgins, Jenny Christensen

Publisher's Cataloging-in-Publication Data

Names: Lajiness, Katie, author.
Title: Kansas City Chiefs / by Katie Lajiness.
Description: Minneapolis, MN : Abdo Publishing, 2017. | Series: NFL's greatest teams | Includes bibliographical references and index.
Identifiers: LCCN 2016944883 | ISBN 9781680785364 (lib. bdg.) | ISBN 9781680798968 (ebook)
Subjects: LCSH: Kansas City Chiefs (Football team)--History--Juvenile literature.
Classification: DDC 796.332--dc23
LC record available at http://lccn.loc.gov/2016944883

Contents

A Winning Team

The Kansas City Chiefs are a football team from Kansas City, Missouri. They have played in the National Football League (NFL) for more than 56 years.

The Chiefs have had good seasons and bad. But time and again, they've proven themselves. Let's see what makes the Chiefs one of the NFL's greatest teams.

Red, gold, and white are the team's colors.

WEST
35
SMITH
11

League Play

Team Standings

The AFC and the National Football Conference (NFC) make up the NFL. Each conference has a north, south, east, and west division.

The NFL got its start in 1920. Its teams have changed over the years. Today, there are 32 teams. They make up two conferences and eight divisions.

Chiefs fans love to show their team spirit!

The Chiefs play in the West Division of the American Football Conference (AFC). This division also includes the Denver Broncos, the Oakland Raiders, and the San Diego Chargers.

The Oakland Raiders have long been a rival of the Chiefs.

Kicking Off

The team started out in Dallas, Texas, in 1960. They were one of the first teams in the American Football League (AFL). At first, the team was called the Dallas Texans.

In 1963, owner Lamar Hunt moved the team to Kansas City. So, the team changed its name to the Kansas City Chiefs.

The Name Game

The original eight cities that formed the AFL were Boston, Buffalo, Dallas, Denver, Houston, Los Angeles, New York City, and Oakland.

The Chiefs name came from Kansas City mayor H. Roe Bartle. His nickname was the Chief.

Highlight Reel

In 1967, the Chiefs played in the first AFL-NFL World **Championship** Game. Sadly, the team lost to the Green Bay Packers. Hunt renamed this game the Super Bowl.

Three years later, the Chiefs played in their second Super Bowl. This time they won! They beat the Minnesota Vikings 23–7.

Win or Go Home

NFL teams play 16 regular season games each year. The teams with the best records are part of the play-off games. Play-off winners move on to the conference championships. Then, conference winners face off in the Super Bowl!

Many people picked the Minnesota Vikings to win the 1970 Super Bowl. But, the Chiefs played better than the Vikings and won the game!

The 1967 AFL-NFL Championship Game was played at the Los Angeles Memorial Coliseum.

In 1972, Hunt became a member of the Pro Football Hall of Fame.

At the start of the 1970 season, the AFL joined with the NFL. The Chiefs struggled during the 1970s and 1980s. They only made it to the play-offs twice.

In 1989, Marty Schottenheimer became head coach. He led the team to success. The Chiefs made it to the play-offs six years in a row.

The Chiefs had a good season in 2015. At first the team lost five straight games. Then they came back and won ten in a row.

Running back Jamaal Charles is the Chiefs all-time leading rusher!

After the 2015 season, the Chiefs made it to the division play-offs. They lost to the New England Patriots 27–20.

Halftime! Stat Break

Team Records

RUSHING YARDS
Career: Jamaal Charles, 7,220 yards (2008–2015)
Single Season: Larry Johnson, 1,789 yards (2006)
PASSING YARDS
Career: Len Dawson, 28,507 yards (1962–1975)
Single Season: Trent Green, 4,591 yards (2004)
RECEPTIONS
Career: Tony Gonzalez, 1,409 receptions (1997–2008)
Single Season: Tony Gonzalez, 102 receptions (2004)
ALL-TIME LEADING SCORER
Nick Lowery, 1,466 points (1980–1993)

Famous Coaches

Hank Stram (1960-1974)
Marty Schottenheimer (1999–2008)

Pro Football Hall of Famers & Their Years with the Chiefs

Bobby Bell, Linebacker/Defensive End (1963–1974)
Junious "Buck" Buchanan, Defensive Tackle (1963–1975)
Curley Culp, Defensive Tackle (1968–1974)
Len Dawson, Quarterback (1962–1975)
Lamar Hunt, League Founder/Owner (1959–2006)
Willie Lanier, Linebacker (1967–1977)
Will Shields, Guard (1993–2006)
Jan Stenerud, Placekicker (1967–1979)
Hank Stram, Coach (1960–1974)
Derrick Thomas, Linebacker (1989–1999)
Emmitt Thomas, Cornerback (1966–1978)

Fan Fun

STADIUM: Arrowhead Stadium
LOCATION: Kansas City, Missouri
MASCOTS: Warpaint and KC Wolf

Championships

SUPER BOWL APPEARANCES:
1967, 1970

SUPER BOWL WINS:
1970

Coaches' Corner

Hank Stram was the team's first head coach. He coached the Chiefs from 1960 to 1974. In 1968, he was named AFL Coach of the Year.

Marty Schottenheimer spent ten seasons as head coach. From 1989 to 1998, he led the team to seven play-off games. In 1993, he coached the Chiefs in their first-ever AFC **championship**.

Stram led the team to its first Super Bowl win!

Coach Andy Reid joined the Chiefs in 2013.

Star Players

Len Dawson QUARTERBACK (1962–1975)

Len Dawson was one of the team's most successful players. He helped the Chiefs win three AFL **championships**. Dawson was voted Most Valuable Player (MVP) of the 1969 Super Bowl. To honor him, the Chiefs no longer use number 16.

Bobby Bell LINEBACKER/DEFENSIVE END (1963–1974)

The Chiefs picked Bobby Bell in the 1963 **draft**. He played in the 1967 and 1970 Super Bowls. Bell played in nine Pro Bowls. This is the NFL's all-star game. In 1983, he was the first Chiefs player to join the Pro Football Hall of Fame.

Jan Stenerud PLACEKICKER (1967–1979)

Jan Stenerud was selected by the Chiefs in the 1966 draft. In 1970, he made a 48-yard field goal during the Super Bowl. Stenerud still holds nine Chiefs records. He was the first placekicker to join the Pro Football Hall of Fame.

Joe Delaney RUNNING BACK (1981–1982)

Joe Delaney's **rookie** year with the Chiefs was great! In 1981, he set a team record by rushing for 1,121 yards. Delaney helped the Chiefs to their first winning season since 1973. The Chiefs named him to their Ring of Honor in 2004.

Derrick Thomas LINEBACKER (1989–1999)

Derrick Thomas was the team's fourth pick in the 1989 **draft**. In his first year, he was named the Defensive Rookie of the Year. Thomas was chosen to play in the Pro Bowl nine times in a row. He played his entire **career** with the Chiefs.

Priest Holmes RUNNING BACK (2001–2007)

Priest Holmes joined the Chiefs in 2001. Over the next three seasons, he was selected to the Pro Bowl each year. While with the chiefs, Holmes recorded 6,070 rushing yards and 76 touchdowns. In 2002, he was named NFL Offensive Player of the Year.

Eric Berry SAFETY (2010–)

Eric Berry was selected as the Chiefs fifth choice in the 2010 NFL **draft**. In 2014, Berry learned he had **cancer**. After he got better, Berry came back for the 2015 season. Berry was also named the 2015 Comeback Player of the Year.

Arrowhead Stadium

The Chiefs play home games at Arrowhead Stadium. It is in Kansas City. The stadium opened in 1972. Arrowhead Stadium was remodeled in 2010. It can hold about 76,000 people.

At home games, fireworks shoot off as players take the field.

Sprint
CHIEFS
O. THOMAS
58

Chiefs Kingdom

Thousands of fans flock to Arrowhead Stadium to see the Chiefs play home games. The fans are known for their loud cheers.

The team's **mascots** are Warpaint and K.C. Wolf. They help fans cheer on the Chiefs at home games.

Earth Shakers

In 2014, fans at Arrowhead stadium yelled really loud. Their noise was similar to the intensity of a jet engine at takeoff!

Susie and Warpaint greet fans before home games. Then they do a victory run when the Chiefs score.

Final Call

The Chiefs have a long, rich history. They won the Super Bowl in 1970.

Even during losing seasons, true fans have stuck by them. Many believe the Kansas City Chiefs will remain one of the greatest teams in the NFL.

Chiefs fans are known for their spirit and fun outfits!

Through the Years

1962

The team wins its first play-off game. The Chiefs beat the Houston Oilers 20–17 in double overtime.

1967

The Chiefs and the Green Bay Packers play in the first-ever Super Bowl. The Chiefs lose 35–10.

1970

The Chiefs win their first Super Bowl.

1972

Linebacker Willie Lanier is the first Chiefs player to receive the NFL Man of the Year award.

2003

The Chiefs score 484 points during the regular season. This is a team record.

2009

The Chiefs, along with other founding members of the AFL, celebrate the AFL's fiftieth anniversary.

1981

Coach Marv Levy writes the Chiefs fight song called "Give a Cheer for Kansas City!"

2015

The team makes a comeback and wins ten straight games to end the season 11–5.

Postgame Recap

1. What was the team's name in 1960?
   A. Dallas Texans **B**. San Antonio Spurs **C**. Houston Rockets

2. What is the name of the stadium where the Chiefs play home games?
   A. AT&T Stadium
   B. Levi's Stadium
   C. Arrowhead Stadium

3. Name 3 of the 11 Chiefs in the Pro Football Hall of Fame.

4. What year did the Chiefs win the Super Bowl?
   A. 1967
   B. 1968
   C. 1970

1. A. 2. C. 3. See page 15. 4. C.

Glossary

cancer any of a group of very harmful diseases that cause a body's cells to become unhealthy.

career a period of time spent in a certain job.

championship a game, a match, or a race held to find a first-place winner.

draft a system for professional sports teams to choose new players.

mascot something to bring good luck and help cheer on a team.

rookie a first-year player in a professional sport.

Websites

To learn more about the NFL's Greatest Teams, visit **booklinks.abdopublishing.com**. These links are routinely monitored and updated to provide the most current information available.

Index